Daddy, Up and Down

Sisters Grieve the Loss of Their Daddy

By Lila Stenson and Anna Stenson
as told to Melanie Friedersdorf Humphrey

Illustrations by Cheryl Biddix

Peaceful Village Publishing
Snowmass Village, CO

**Peaceful
Village
Publishing**

To my mom and dad and my brother Jack.
--LMS

To my mom.
--AMS

In honor of Bill and Meg
and their beautiful children.
--MFH

For my Aunt Ronda, Derek and Angela;
and in memory of my uncle, Ray Ulrich.
--CLB

Printed in the United States of America
by Walsworth Publishing Company

First edition, 2002

Peaceful Village Publishing
P.O. Box 7032
Snowmass Village, CO 81615

ISBN 0-9658061-1-1
Library of Congress Control Number: 2002106178

Cover design and page layout by Mickey Gill
Editor, Heidi Ferré

The text of this book is set in Goudy.
The original illustrations are cut paper collage.

"a father to the fatherless, the widow's defender--God in his holy dwelling-place."
Psalms 68:05

In the weeks following their father's death on December 29, 1999, Lila and Anna Stenson frequently asked their mother Meg if there were any other children like themselves whose daddy had died. As my husband John and I watched the tragedy of September 11, 2001 unfold and faced the realities, I tearfully said to him, "Now there are too many children like Lila, Anna, and Jack."

Only weeks later, Meg called and asked me if I would help Lila and Anna write a book, because, in their own words, they wanted, "to help other children who had lost their daddies or mommies." May I say that it has been an honor to work with the girls. I hope that this book does, indeed, help. The feelings and words are theirs.

Melanie Friedersdorf Humphrey
May 2002

Lila and Anna's daddy died.

Lila was four and a half years old and Anna was three.
Their brother Jack had just been born.

Lila and Anna want to help other children
who have lost their daddy or mommy.

They want them to know that
it is okay to feel sad and even angry.
Sometime

heir mom and grandparents feel sad and angry, too.

After two years, Anna still wants to be sad. She doesn't like feeling angry, though, and she doesn't like anyone to say that word, "angry."

Even though she is sad,
Lila sometimes feels happy now.
It can seem weird to have two different feelings, but it is normal to feel that way.

Lila smiles when she talks about her daddy.

She likes to tell people that her daddy
was the coach for her soccer team
and that they loved to ride bikes together.
And she wants you to know that, even
if you lost your daddy, you can't really

know how she and Anna feel, because you didn't lose their daddy.

Sometimes it is hard for Lila and Anna
to say that they are sad.

It is so hard to believe that
someone you love can die.

It is hard to believe that the person
will never come back to life to ride bikes with
you and go swimming with you
and tuck you in at night.

After their daddy died,
Lila and Anna worried that something
could happen to their mom, too.

Their mom was also very sad.
And she was very busy taking care of all of them
and trying to do the things tha

...eir daddy used to do.

Lila and Anna needed people they could talk to. They needed to let them know that they felt sad and angry, and that they missed their daddy very much.

Sometimes it felt good just to be with a friend and to play.

When they show their brother pictures of their
daddy and ask him whe

Lila and Anna have told him that daddy's
soul is up in heaven and his
body is in the ground.

When they think about their daddy,
Lila and Anna remember the
things that made their daddy special.
They think about the way
he laughed and giggled.
They remember his smile.
They think about his feelings.

Lila and Anna have had two parades
and a running race to honor their daddy.
They got the idea for a parade

Their mommy told them that
Dr. King was a great man,
and that was the reason for the parade.

They said,
"Our daddy was a really great man, too!"

when they went to one for Martin Luther King, Jr.

He was.

After the race for their daddy,
the girls gave everyone
a balloon and said,
"Think of our daddy
when you let go of this."

Lila and Anna gave the word, and everyone

(except Anna) let go of his balloon.

The balloons soared high up in the sky.
And everyone thought
about Lila and Anna's daddy
and how his soul was up there, too.

And, even though they were sad,
Lila and Anna felt happy because
their daddy's spirit was in their hearts,
and their memories of him
were with them...

and they always will be.

Mommy☺

Meg Jack Lilo

Anna

We ♥ Daddy

Note to parents, caregivers, and educators:

This book was begun almost two years after Bill Stenson died on December 29, 1999. Bill was only thirty-six years old when he died unexpectedly. His wife Meg was thirty-five and their children, Lila, Anna, and Jack, were four and a half, three, and three months old. Lila has been seeing a child therapist since Bill's death. Anna has been seeing a different therapist since she turned four and a half. Meg visits with both therapists regularly, and she would like to emphasize the importance of counseling or psychotherapy after losing a family member.

Meg also wants you to know that for each member of her family, feelings have changed, and continue to change. Family members—especially children—do not necessarily move through the grieving process at the same pace. Children's emotions and understanding change as they develop. And, it is difficult for children to express their feelings unless they also see a parent or role model expressing his own.

Please read this book with your child and allow time for questions and discussion afterward. If possible, use examples in nature to discuss death with your children before they lose a grandparent, parent, or loved one. Continue to discuss death as your child ages, matures, and develops. And, of course, treasure those you love each day.
                                        —MFH